Wild flowers of New York

(1912)

ISBN-13 : 978-1511555760

ISBN-10 : 1511555769

Notice

This documentary study use historic, archived documents.

Because of this, some pages may look blurry or low quality.

Still are included in this book because they have

high value from critical, documentary, historical,

informative and journalistic point of view .

Dtp
and
visual art

Iacob Adrian

This little Book conveys the greetings of

....

to

....

_____

WILD ROSE

WILD FLOWERS

Flowering plants are numbered by the thousands; consequently in the book we are able to include only some of the more important and most beautiful species. There are all kinds of plants, some good and some useless. Some furnish foods, others are of great value medicinally, still others furnish coloring matter for dyes, and quantities of them have a large aesthetic value; on the other hand many are poisonous, some deadly so, and quantities are absolutely useless weeds that spring up readily and in great quantities to the detriment of agricultural products.

Most species that bear conspicuous flowers do so for their own good and not simply to look pretty. They are designed to attract certain insects that are necessary or useful to assist them in setting seed. As will be seen in the illustration on the following page, flowers have stamens and pistils, the tips of the former bearing anthers containing pollen grains and the end of the latter, called the stigma, being sticky and connecting through a slender tube through the style to the ovary in the basal portion. In order that seed may set, it is necessary that pollen should come in contact with the stigma. If seed was always set by pollen from the same flower, the continuous inbreeding would in time cause the species to degenerate. To prevent this, many plants are incapable of setting seed unless pollen is brought from some other flower. Insects are the chief agents for performing this duty and a great many ingenious devices force them to do so if they wish to partake of the nectar that the flowers provide as compensation for their services. No branch of science offers a wider field or a more interesting one than the methods of plant reproduction.

Just as interesting are the many devices intended to prevent useless insects from pilfering the nectar, such as hairy or sticky stems or parts to prevent crawling insects from reaching the flowers, long nectar tubes within which short-tongued flies and bees cannot reach, etc.

Sepal · Petal · Stigma · Anther · Style · Pollen · Ovary · Filament · CALYX · COROLLA · PISTIL · STAMEN · Petiole · Rays · Peduncle · Disc · Bract · Composite Head · Disc Flower · Ray Flower · Bell-shaped · Funnel-shaped · Rosaceous · Hood · Limb · Lip · Salver shaped · Spadix · Labiate · Papilionaceous · Spathe · Umbel · Panicle · Spike · Raceme · Corymb · Axillary flowers

PARTS AND FORMS OF FLOWERS

JACK-IN-THE-PULPIT.

This, our best known representative of the Arum family, is very abundant during spring in moist woodlands. As its form shows, it is a very close relative of the exquisite Calla Lily. The handsomely striped and veined exterior of what is often considered the flower is known as a spathe, and is the pulpit from which Jack, represented by the vertically projecting spadix, is supposed to preach. The real flowers are small and greenish-yellow, clustered about the base of this spadix or smooth, glossy green column. Some of these plants have clusters of both staminate and pistillate flowers and are self-fertilizing, but most of them have either the one kind or the other and require the assistance of insects in transferring pollen from the one to the other.

Some plants are so constructed as to welcome with open arms the insects that are useful to them and to exclude all others. Let us see how Jack treats his many visitors. The column and the inside of the spathe are very slippery, and the former has an abrupt enlargement in the middle leaving just room between it and the sides so that visitors can easily slide down the polished surface but can neither crawl back nor find room to extend their wings in flight. If not too large and they happen to find it, there is a small opening in the lower flap of the spathe through which they may force their way; insects so escaping, their bodies perhaps dusted with pollen, forget the trap and immediately enter another plant, perhaps a pistillate one and fulfill the designs of our Jack, but at the cost of the lives of others not so fortunate in finding the avenue of escape from the prison.

The name Indian Turnip is often applied to this plant since Indians used to boil and eat the acrid, turnip-like roots.

TURK'S-CAP LILY; TIGER LILY.

None of our several species of lilies are more beautiful, more graceful or decorative than the Turk's-cap. With stately grandeur some of the stalks rise to heights of six or seven feet and terminate in the most brilliant array of pendent blossoms varying in number from two or three up to forty. They usually grow closely together in colonies, forming masses of brilliant color that can be seen to best advantage in low meadows along railroad lines during July and August.

In full bloom, the six points of the perianth of this species are curved far back, while those of the Canada or Wild Yellow Lily are always spreading or bell-shaped. Another beautiful species known as the Red Wood Lily, but which grows most commonly in moist sandy ground, has the deep red bell-shaped perianth turned upward instead of being in a pendulous position.

The brightly colored lilies are fertilized by bees or butterflies which are attracted by brilliant colors while the white ones cater to the long-tongued night moths or sphinges. Anyone who has ever handled these lilies knows how easily the pollen is rubbed from the large anthers and can readily see that a visiting bee, searching for the nectar that is contained in grooves at the base of the flower, can scarcely avoid becoming powdered with it. As he visits the next bloom, even while getting a fresh dose of pollen on his under parts, he is leaving some of that from the previous one on the sticky, projecting stigma. The long stems, thickly studded with leaves make upward progress very arduous for crawling insects and the deep recesses within which the nectar is contained prevent short-tongued ones from reaching the sweets.

WILD SPIKENARD.

In rich, uncleared ground or thickets this species, which also belongs to the Lily Family, grows in abundance. The angular stem, which grows from one to three feet in length, is alternately set with large, wavy-edged pointed leaves and, during May and June, is terminated with a flowering spike, each tiny white flower of which has a perfectly formed six-parted perianth.

Later in the year a cluster of small purple or magenta berries is to be seen in place of the white blossoms. This berry-method of dispersing the seeds is one used by a great many plants and is very successful. Birds eating the berries often carry the seeds for miles from the place of their growth before dropping them.

Somewhat similar to Spikenard in form and arrangement of stem and leaves is the well known Solomon's Seal which grows abundantly in all rich woods. If we pull up one of the roots we may easily understand the name; the thick perennial rootstock is scarred and sealed in many places, each representing the seat of the plant stem of a previous year. The flowers of Solomon's Seal are little greenish bells suspended in pairs below the leaves at their junctions with the main stem.

Still another form of lily grows along the banks of woodland streams or brooks, a small dainty species usually known as the Dog-tooth Violet or yellow Adder's-tongue. The name violet of course is a misnomer for it is a true lily with the usual perfect six-parted, bell-like perianth. The single straw-colored blossom grows, nodding from a slender stem rising from between two clasping spotted leaves. It is often appropriately termed the Trout Lily because it blooms along trout brooks and again known as the Fawn Lily, because of the leaves, which are green, spotted with purple and white.

CANADA MAYFLOWER.

Whole woods, particularly coniferous ones, are often carpeted with the low growing green leaves of this plant which is shown on the left in the picture. The flower on the right is the Three-leaved False Solomon's Seal; the two species are often confused with one another but a close examination will show that the flowers of the former have a four-parted perianth while those of the latter are divided into six points besides being fewer in number. Either species may have two or three leaves, so the number cannot be used as a guide to their identity.

They bloom most profusely about Memorial Day and as the leaves are so clean and bright and the flowers so beautiful and dainty, they are used quite extensively for decorating. During fall the place of each pistillate flower is occupied by a small purple berry, standing erect and awaiting the appearance of the bird which is destined to carry its precious seed-contents to other localities. Thus birds not only play a very important part in the economy of nature by destroying injurious insects, but also assist in the distribution of our plant life to a very considerable extent.

The true Lily of the Valley, while very familiar as a cultivated species is wild only in the mountains of our southern states. It is, however, often found in New York and New England as an escape from gardens. The delicate little, nodding, white bell-shaped flowers grow along the upper part of a slender stem, rising from the bases of two large, oval pointed leaves. The leaf veins, like those of nearly all species belonging to this family, run lengthwise of the leaf.

PAINTED TRILLIUM.

The trilliums derive their name from the fact that all their parts are arranged in threes—three leaves, three petals, three sepals and a three-parted stigma. The Painted Trillium, which is the handsomest species has its waxy-white, wavy-edged flower standing erect above the whorl of three leaves. It is quite abundant in certain moist woodland and often grows in large beds.

Two other white species are quite abundant, the large-flowered White Trillium which has blossoms two or three inches across and the Nodding Trillium, which has smaller white flowers suspended, inverted, below the whorl of leaves. Neither of these species have the crimson mark that adds so much to the beauty of the Painted variety.

Beautiful as they are, all the trilliums have a slight disagreeable odor while that of the Purple Trillium or Wake Robin is very unpleasant, strongly resembling the odor of decomposing flesh. Presumably, this odor is for the purpose of alluring certain carrion flies to the flowers, which insects are the chief fertilizing agents. In the case of the Purple Trillium, the color too is one that would attract flies that were in the habit of seeking out putrid substances. This species flowers in April and May, which early flowering is one of the reasons for the name of Wake Robin, although, as a matter of fact, they do not bloom until weeks after robins have arrived in abundance.

After the flowering season a single, oval berry is seated above and close to the whorled leaves.

YELLOW STAR GRASS.

From the latter part of April, throughout the summer, the handsome golden stars of this common plant gleam at us from the grass carpeted ground of pasture or first growth woods. It belongs to the Amaryllis Family, a small family closely related to the Lilies, having flat grass-like leaves and long slender stems bearing six-parted flowers. The leaves of the present species so closely resemble grass that the plants would not be noticed were it not for the blossoms. The flower is wide spread and of six equal divisions. Although half a dozen or more buds are in a loose umbel at the top of each stem, the flowers open but one or two at a time, so that the period of bloom for each plant may extend over a period of many days. The blossoms yield little or no nectar but are visited by many smaller bees for pollen, some of which is unavoidably carried on their bodies and deposited on the sticky stigmas of blossoms visited later, thus effecting cross-fertilization that is so vital to the continued healthy existence of many plants.

In moist fields and meadows another flowering grass-like plant is commonly found, namely Blue-eyed Grass which belongs to the Iris Family. The leaves are very narrow and the stem long, slender, angular and sometimes prostrate—quite uninteresting were it not for the beautiful six-parted flowers with their bright golden centers and violet petals, very appropriately termed blue-eyed.

The blossoms are very sensitive and remain open for but a single day and only on bright days at that. While the sun shines the pretty blue eyes will twinkle at you but towards the close of day, they close in sleep never to open again, but their places on the morrow will be taken by new faces.

BLUE FLAG; IRIS.

Just the thought of Iris always recalls pleasant pictures to the mind, visions of a pond with its unruffled mirroring surface; the blackbirds that protest so vigorously when you are near their basket-like nests hanging just over the water; the frogs that dive with a great splash into its bosom as we tread the edges; the turtles which are lazily sunning themselves on an old stump; the heron that starts up with a single shriek of warning and slowly flaps away to more remote fishing grounds; the rattle of the kingfisher which you have disturbed perhaps just as he was about to pounce upon a fish to carry to his clamoring young in yonder bank; the swaying rushes and cat-tails sheltering the noisy and boisterous Marsh Wren; the dragon-flies that go darting hither and yon hawking after the many species of insects that are to be found over still water; and the great clumps of Blue Flags that add a touch of bright color and cheer to the whole picture.

We are accustomed to think of the petals as the most attractive part of a flower, but in this case it is the sepals that are enlarged, bright colored and attract our attention. The name Iris, which is quite appropriate, is from the Greek meaning rainbow and surely the coloring of the sepals on this species may readily suggest the rainbow. The flowers are so constructed that fertilization from their own pollen is impossible, the anthers being located under and below the stigmas which are at the end of the petal-like division of the style. It is a well established fact that certain insects are most strongly attracted by certain colors and the blues and purples are favorites of honey bees. It is these bees that visit the Iris and are the chief agents of its fertilization.

SHOWY LADY'S SLIPPER.

Lady's Slippers belong to that most remarkable of plant families, the Orchids. Orchids are noted for the peculiarity of their blossoms which sometimes take very grotesque shapes. Usually one or more of the petals or sepals are greatly enlarged into a sac, a broad platform or are curiously slashed and subdivided. They are the most highly specialized of all flowers, each dependant upon the agency of certain insects to insure their fertilization, some dependant upon the visit of just one species of insect; if that one does not appear, no new seed will be set; only a few years of failure will result in the species being lost to that locality.

The expedient most often adopted by orchids to prevent useless insects from pilfering the bountiful supply of nectar is to have it at the end of a long slender tube or spur; only a long-tongued insect can reach the sweet and it will be found that the one that is best fitted for the purpose is the one that is also adapted to best accomplish the fertilization of the blossom. For instance the large White-fringed Orchid is visited by a sphinx moth, which has a tongue of just the right length to drain the nectary. As he presses his face into the tube to reach the last drop his eyes come into contact with tiny sticky buttons to which the pollen masses are attached; as he withdraws his head the pollen masses are drawn from their pockets and project forward, one from either eye. Since the moth eye is a large compound one, the covering of part of the surface does not seriously inconvenience him; he flies away to the next blossom and lo—the pollen masses are in just the right position to be pressed into the stigma of that flower. Some of these processes of fertilization are very complicated ones and are very interesting to study.

PINK LADY'S SLIPPER; MOC-
CASIN FLOWER.

This species is the most widely distributed and one of the most abundant species. The single blossom tops a long stem that grows from two clasping leaves at the base. Our other species have leafy stems, that is the leaves alternate up the stem almost to the flower. The largest and most magnificent variety is the Showy Lady's Slipper, shown on the preceding page; the blossoms are also quite fragrant. Another species, the Small White Lady's Slipper, is not only smaller but lacks the crimson touches that so beautify this one. Rather rare, except in our higher portions, are the small Yellow Lady's Slippers, with their curiously bent and twisted brown sepals.

Pink Lady's Slippers are locally met with in small colonies in rath'r dry woods. The large, delicate pink blossoms are fertilized through the agency of bumblebees. He enters through the closed fissure in front, his strength being sufficient to force his way in; after eating his fill he takes the easiest way out, through the top; as he forces his burly frame through the narrowing passage his back brushes against a sticky stigma removing any pollen that may have been brought from the previous blossom visited; as he continues, just before emerging, an anther blocks his passage and claps a fresh load of pollen on his back in readiness to continue the good work.

Our bumblebee is one of the most useful insects that we have, performing the same duties to many species of plants. Very fortunately, he makes the rounds of flowers of the same kind, thereby avoiding the waste of brushing pollen from one species of plant off on another. Mutilated Lady's Slippers are often caused by large bees, which bite their way through the wall rather than force out in the proper manner.

WATER-LILY.

The chaste purity and beauty of our large white Water-Lilies, pictured on the lower half of this illustration, cannot be excelled and their sweet fragrance in unequaled by that of any other species. Although the early Water-Lilies are picked in great numbers and sold on the streets of our cities at so much per bunch, their period of bloom is so long and so many seeds are set from each blossom that remains, that their numbers do not decrease materially except in very restricted areas. The floating leaves are large, four to twelve inches across, attached to the rootstock by very long, round, hollow stems. The flowers have four greenish sepals, many waxy-white petals and a center of many yellow stamens. They open early in the morning, remain open at least during sunshine and close at night. They are fertilized chiefly by small flies and bees, many of which are attracted by the fragrance and the conspicuous bloom.

The joys of paddling a canoe along watery lanes dotted with these magnificent flowers cannot be experienced by everyone, but there is consolation in the fact that these hardy Water-lilies can be successfully grown in our own yards. Many residents in our cities have their lily ponds or tubs on their lawns; they are particularly desirable for decorative purposes since they are in bloom from the first of June until September and species of different shades, white, pink, red and blue, can be secured. An added pleasure is secured by introducing a few goldfish into the little pond, both for appearance and to prevent the breeding of mosquitoes.

The upper picture illustrates the Yellow Pond Lily or Cow Lily, a species that grows abundantly in many ponds, particularly in stagnant water.

WOOD ANEMONE; WIND FLOWER.

This species, shown on the left of the picture, is exceedingly delicate in appearance but appearances are often deceptive for, frail as it seems, it blooms in April and early May. Swayed this way and that, with a violence that threatens to demolish it, it safely weathers the most severe storms and with the appearance of the sun its nodding head beckons a welcome to the early bees. Very appropriate indeed is its most common name of Wind Flower. The single flower head rises above a whorl of three five-parted leaves that top a slender stem; the four to seven sepals are pure white within but purplish white on the outside; they would spread about an inch, but are rarely seen fully expanded, usually hanging bell-like. The stem grows from a horizontal rootstock.

RUE ANEMONE.

This species is smaller in every respect than the Wind Flower. Both kinds grow in our woods, often side by side. Rue Anemone has a very slender and delicate stem growing from a little cluster of tuberous roots; the whorl of leaves is more than three in number and each leaf has a heart-shaped base and is three-lobed; instead of a single blossom, several flowers rise on slender stalks above the leaves.

Tall Meadow Rue is an ambitious, bushy looking plant that rears its filmy flower heads from two to five feet above ground in swamps or along streams. The long-stemmed leaves are many times compounded into small three-lobed leaflets; the flowers are in feathery clusters, each composed of many long stamens and no petals, but having usually four, early-falling sepals.

WILD COLUMBINE.

In spring, Wild Columbine greets us on rocky hillsides and in dry woods, its handsome pendent blossoms nodding a welcome to every breath of air. Columbine is a hardy species under cultivation but, although the blossoms attain a larger size, they lack the very daintiness that appeals to us in the wild plant. The slender, wiry, branching stem is set with three-parted leaves; but it is the blossoms that droop from the thread-like peduncles that interest us the most— bright red outside and yellow within; each of the five petals is funnel-shaped, terminated with a spur and extending backward from between the projecting sepals. Nectar is contained in the tips of the slender spurs and it must undoubtedly be a long-tongued creature that is able to drain the cups legitimately. Small bees, that are unable to get at the nectar in the proper way, are wise enough to gnaw through the spurs and steal the sweets. The big bumblebee, however, swings back down from the swaying flower with all the abandon of the trained gymnast on his trapeze and drinks to his heart's content. Yet this is not the creature for which the Columbine is waiting, although the large bees can fertilize the flowers. If we are fortunate we may see the visitor for which the flower flaunts its flaming red advertisement; with a buzz of wings a tiny Hummingbird appears and. hovering before each blossom, quickly inserts his bill successively in the cornucopias. Red is the favorite color of our Hummingbird and whenever you see a long-tubed red flower, you may be quite certain that the smallest of birds will sooner or later visit it.

Goldthread, shown on the right of the same plate, is a small woodland plant, so named because of the bright yellow, threadlike roots.

CELANDINE.

Although this is a stranger in a strange land, having come to our shores from across the seas, it has thriven and multiplied with the rapidity common to aliens and extended its range to include the whole eastern half of the United States.

The stem is quite stout and very branching. At the end of each branch is a loose cluster of buds on slender stems; these open one or two at a time commencing in May and continuing to bloom all summer. The flowers are half an inch or more broad; with four golden-yellow petals, a long, slender, pointed green pistil  and numerous yellow stamens. Towards the end of the season, the continued flowering is marked by a large number of long slender seed pods; when fully ripened the pods split at the base and allow the escape of the seeds.

The thin, soft leaves are divided into three to seven handsome scalloped leaflets. Both stem and leaves have very acrid, yellow juices that stain everything they come in contact with. Celandine grows in abundance in waste land, in rich moist woodland and along beds of brooks.

During April and May, in rich hilly woods, we may sometimes find the peculiar plant known as Dutchman's Breeches. The reason for the name is readily apparent to those who have seen the little white trousers dangling along the slender flowering stalk, which rises from five to nine inches above ground. The leaves are very much divided and slashed and all rise from the rootstock on long stems. Dutchman's Breeches belongs to the Fumitory Family, all species of which have finely divided leaves and smooth rather slender stems which contain watery juices.

PITCHER PLANT.

The Pitcher Plant is our most interesting representative of so-called carnivorous or insectivorous plants. It belongs to a small family of bog-inhabiting plants having hollow leaves. Peat bogs and spongy, mossy swamps are its favorite haunts, and to such places we must go during late May or June if we are to see the unusual and handsome blossoms. Each individual flower hangs in an inverted position from the top of a long slender hollow scape growing from the root. They are unusual both in form and coloring as the accompanying picture shows. Interesting as the flowers are, it is the leaves that must claim the most of our attention—hollow pitchers radiating in all directions. They are nearly always partially filled with water, some of which must be rain water received through the opening and some of which is a natural fluid secreted by the plant. This fluid is sweet and some claim intoxicating while others say it acts as an anaesthetic. In either case it is quite fatal to the insect endeavoring to partake of it. Entrance to the pitcher is easy over the hairs which all point downward, around the brim; once beyond these, the creature slides down the slippery side to the water and is unable to crawl back or to fly upward once the wings have become wet. Decomposing bodies of many species of insects are often to be found in these pitchers, the resulting products being absorbed by the plant.

The Pitcher Plant drowns its victims but our Sundews, which are common in sandy soil and often along roadsides, entangle theirs in the tiny sticky drops that exude from the tips of the many hairs covering the surface of the rounded leaves; the leaf then slowly furls and actually digests its victim by means of its gastric juices.

WILD STRAWBERRY.

(Shown by A in the opposite picture)

HIGH BUSH BLACKBERRY.

(Shown by B in the opposite picture)

These two plants need no introduction and are only included because they are so very common and so popular that to omit them would be an almost unpardonable offense in the eyes of the school children who gather the luscious strawberries from the low vines that trail through many of our fields, or the equally delectable blackberry that is to be found in thickets, along walls or by the roadside and whose thorns are often the cause of severe reproof of the parents when the child returns with frock or trousers sadly in need of repairs.

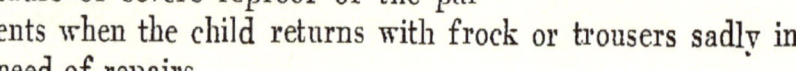

Strawberries and blackberries belong to the Rose Family, a large family containing a very great many species of widely differing plants, but all agreeing in the feature of having five petals and five sepals. Presumably to protect themselves from browsing mammals, many species which dwell in open or pasture land are armed with sharp prickles.

One of our most common roses, the Wild Swamp Rose, is shown in our frontispiece. All our wild roses are what we call single, that is they have but the correct number of petals—five. The beautiful monstrocities (I am using this term only in the sense of their being so widely at variance with the original forms) produced by our gardeners and horticulturists are nearly all originated from foreign species. Roses secrete no nectar but furnish an abundance of pollen for the numerous bees, flies and beetles that visit them.

CINQUEFOIL; FIVE-FINGER.

The left hand picture shows the common Cinquefoil, the one that spreads so abundantly over fields and pastures, while on the right is Silvery Cinquefoil, so called because of the silvery appearance of the under surfaces of the leaves. The latter species is most common in dry barren ground, especially near the coast.

The common Cinquefoil is regarded as a pernicious weed since it spreads so rapidly by means of its creeping stem. It is often mistaken for the Wild Strawberry or called the yellow flowered strawberry. There is a yellow flowered Barren Strawberry that grows profusely on our hillsides and in small woods but it is easily recognized by the pretty trifoliate leaves that carpet the ground, often in the same localities as Cinquefoil.

STEEPLEBUSH or HARDHACK also belongs to the rose family although one would not suspect it at a casual glance. Yet each tiny pink flower has all the rose characters except size. It is a very attractive plant or shrub standing erect, from two to five feet tall, with reddish-brown stem closely set with handsome leaves which are dark green above and light on the under surfaces, the whole topped off with the delicately colored spire-like flower cluster. The flowers blossom from the summit downward and the period of bloom is so long continued that by the time the lower flowers are fully opened the upper ones are faded and brownish in color. These small flowers secrete little or no nectar but have an abundance of pollen and are consequently visited by pollen eating bees and flies. These visitors cannot avoid carrying pollen from plant to plant and shaking it from upper flowers to receptive stigmas of flowers below. Hardhack grows most abundant in low land but also in moist situations at any elevation.

STONE or RABBIT'S-FOOT CLOVER.

(Shown by A in the opposite picture)
COMMON RED CLOVER.

(Shown by B in the opposite picture)

Clovers, which are among our best known and most valuable plants, are characterized by their three-parted or trifoliate leaves and rather round flower heads. A very common species and the most noticeable one because of the size and color of the flower heads, is Red Clover. It is present in nearly every field, meadow, pasture and yard and is visited by a great many handsome butterflies as well as several species of bees. It is said to be so dependant upon our common bumblebee for fertilization that without the aid of this insect, the clover soon perishes. The little pink florets, which compose the flower head are sweet scented and abound in nectar. The whitish inverted V-shaped mark in the middle of each leaflet adds much to the beauty of the plant.

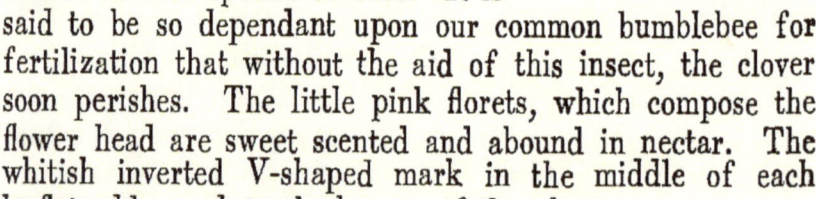

WHITE CLOVER is a smaller plant in every way, but the white or pale pink florets that make up the smaller flower head are very fragrant. This species is one of the most useful for honey bees and also furnishes excellent fodder for cattle, large fields being often sown to it for both purposes. It also roots very readily and makes a good foundation for lawns; hence clover seed is usually sown with grass seed for the making of new lawns.

RABBIT'S-FOOT CLOVER is a small but very attractive species that abounds everywhere. The small elongated flower heads are very soft and silky owing to the long, pinkish feathery tips to the five-parted calices. They are visited by the smallest of butterflies, particularly by the handsome species usually known as the Little Copper Butterfly.

WOOD SORRELS.

Wood Sorrels are handsome but very dainty and delicate plants, the WHITE WOOD SORREL (shown by A in the opposite picture) being very abundant in cool, shady recesses of mountainous regions where the handsome leaves often carpet the ground in large patches. The leaves are quite clover-like but are broadly heart shaped at the ends of the leaflets. They are so very sensitive that they fold up every night, during cloudy or stormy weather and also upon being touched. The juices of the plant are very sour, in fact Oxalic acid. which is so often used for removing the stains of iron rust from clothing, is made from the leaves of this very species, which is native to Europe and Africa. During June, white, pink veined, five-petalled flowers appear, one on each stalk, above the green leaves.

VIOLET WOOD SORREL is very similar except that the flowers are colored as shown in B on the picture on this page and two or more blossoms appear from the top of each flower stalk. This species is not nearly as abundant as the preceding one.

WILD GERANIUM or CRANESBILL is found growing abundantly in most open woodland and thickets. Both the flowers and leaves of this plant are strikingly handsome, the former being quite large and showy, with five, rounded, delicately veined rose-purple petals, and ten violet-tipped stamens surrounding a curious elongated green pistil which gives the plant the name of Cranesbill. This pistil is the pods in which the seeds develop and when matured, it splits suddenly sending the seeds sharply in all directions, this being one of the plants that adopts the "spring-gun" method for distributing its seeds. The leaves are large and coarsely veined, five-cleft and notched and slashed. The flowers are quite fragile. drooping soon after being plucked and the petals fall off upon the slightest provocation.

YELLOW WOOD SORREL; LADY'S SORREL.

This species is not a woodland plant but blooms abundantly in fields, gardens and along roadsides as well. From April until October the bright yellow blossoms show their shining faces above the frail leaves; they open only during sunshine and close each night, at which time the leaves also fold up umbrella-fashion. The sensitive leaves are quite acrid, having a flavor very similar to those of the leaves of the common Red Sorrel.

FRINGED POLYGALA or MILKWORT is a pretty little plant growing in rich moist woods or swamps. The leaves and form of the plant are somewhat like that of the common Wintergreen, but the leaves are more pointed at the tips. The pretty pink flowers that appear during May and June are quite orchid-like, three of the petals forming a central tube enclosing the stamens and the other two wide spreading like wings, and suggesting to children the title of "Bird-on-the-wing" by which they often know the plant. They also bear tiny underground flowers that are self-fertilizing, while the outer ones, which are borne in pairs, are dependent upon bees for transferring pollen to their stigmas.

FIELD or PURPLE MILKWORT is a sturdy little pink-headed plant that grows in fields or along roadsides in company with Hop or Yellow Clover and it is a singular fact that the flowers of these two plants belonging to distinct families should be similar in form. The leafy stem which grows from six to twelve inches tall, branches at the top and each branch terminates in a cylindrical flower head, the flowers proper being concealed beneath the pink, scale-like sepals that closely overlap one another. The bloom is from the bottom of the head upward, the lower rows maturing and dropping away as the flowering continues.

The name Polygala is derived from the Greek, meaning much milk and was given these plants since it was believed cattle feeding upon them gave more plentifully.

JEWEL-WEED or SPOTTED TOUCH-ME-NOT.

Jewel-weed grows in rank, almost tropical profusion in moist ground, particularly about the edges of ponds or along watercourses. The reason for its name is not difficulty to understand when one sees the funny little orange cornucopias hanging from their slender stems like jewels pendent from a lady's ear in the olden days. There are many, however, who claim a different origin for the name; perhaps they are right,—we cannot say. The thin toothed leaves have a peculiar texture that sheds water; after a rain or heavy dew, we will see glistening drops collected along the margins of the leaves and it does not even require a fertile imagination to see in them, jewels such as only Nature can produce.

This plant grows from two to five feet in height, having a reddish, smooth branching stem along which the leaves alternate. The flowers hang in pairs from the axils of the outer leaves, although usually but one of them opens at a time. The peculiar flower has three petals and three sepals, one of the latter forming the crooked sac in the base of which nectar is concealed. While some bees and moths are able to get at the nectar, apparently Hummingbirds which visit the blossoms frequently are the benefactors for which the plant is catering. However seed will be set, even if neither bird nor insects visit the blossoms, for Jewel-weed bears also cleistogamous flowers that never open and which fertilize themselves.

The plant is of more than passing interest even after the flowering season because of the curiously twisted seed pods that take the places of the blossoms. When these are ripened, the slightest touch causes them to instantly split and coil so quickly as to send the seeds flying two or three feet in every direction. Even though we know just what is going to happen, one cannot help being startled at the very suddenness of the "explosion."

ROSE MALLOW.

The Rose Mallow is one of the most strikingly beautiful plants to be found in our range, but it grows, except very locally, only in slightly brackish marshes or swamps along our Atlantic seaboard. The stout-stemmed plant grows from three to seven feet in height and has very large leaves, from three to eight inches in length. But it is the magnificent blossoms that attract our attention,—mammoth pink beauties measuring four to eight inches across. The stamens are united into a large column, bearing anthers on the exterior surface; the pistil projects through and beyond this column. The newly opened flowers in which the pollen is ripened, are wide spread so that bees may get at the nectar at the base and get pollen on their backs without coming into contact with the yet unripened stigmas; but they carry this pollen to older flowers which are partially folded and in trying to get by the five stigmas that partially block the entrance cannot avoid dusting some of the precious grains on the sticky surfaces.

MARSH MALLOW, the plant from the roots of which the mucilagenous substance so much used in confectionary is made, belongs to a different genus from the Rose Mallow. It is not common here but has been naturalized from Europe in a few places near the coast. Its pink flowers are much smaller than those of the preceding species, being not more than an inch and a half across.

The COMMON MALLOW is an abundant weed about old farm houses and along some country roads. Country school children are very familiar with it for it furnishes them with the so-called "cheeses" that they delight in eating. It is a low and spreading plant having rather pretty notched and lobed leaves and small pale blue or white flowers, measuring barely half an inch across.

BLUE VIOLETS.

On the left in the opposite picture is shown the COMMON, PURPLE or MEADOW VIOLET, one of the most delightful species and one that grows in profusion everywhere. In dry fields we find the plants small and the blossoms low down so as to be partly shielded by the grass; in meadows and marshes, the leaves and the flowers have exceedingly long stems, but in cool, shady, moist woods we find the plants in their most perfect form and proportion. Violets are favorite flowers with everyone; they lack only a sweet scent to make them ideal. So many violets are collected every year to make nosegays for the young ladies that it is very fortunate that they are not entirely dependent upon the visible flowers setting seed, or the species would become very rare. That it does not diminish in numbers is due to the fact that at the base, sometimes underground are tiny flowers that never open and that fertilize themselves and produce seed. Of course enough of the showy flowers are cross fertilized by bees to keep the plants from degenerating by continued inbreeding. These violets are often transplanted to the garden or raised in hothouses, in the latter case the blossoms sometimes attain a somewhat larger size than they do even under the most favorable conditions outside. The present species, which is technically known as Viola cucullata, has the heart-shaped leaves all growing from the base on long slender petioles. Another common blue violet, the CANADA VIOLET (V. canadensis), shown by the picture on the right hand, has a leafy stem and the flowers raised on slender stems rising from the axils of the leaves. Still another species, very abundant in the southern states and of local occurrence in our range, known as BIRD-FOOT VIOLET (V. pedata), has the leaves which proceed from the base, deeply cut into from five to eleven parts. This species also has unusually large bright orange anthers blocking the entrance to the flower throat.

WHITE VIOLETS.

Although not nearly as showy and conspicuous as their larger blue and purple cousins, SWEET WHITE VIOLETS have an attraction that the others do not have in that they are sweet scented. Like the blue ones, they grow small and short in unfavorable situations and long-stemmed and fairly large in the marshes or moist woods that are their preferable haunts. The flowers are small, expanding less than a half inch. Fine purplish lines running down the throat guide visiting insects to the nectary at the base of the short spur. Smaller and shorter tongued bees and butterflies usually visit the white violets, while those with comparatively long tongues only, can reach to the bottom of the longer spurs on the blue violets. The leaves of this species, all proceeding from the base of the plant, are heart-shaped at the base but much rounder than those of the Common Blue Violet.

The LANCE-LEAVED VIOLET, also a white species, is taller and more slender than the Sweet White variety and the flowers are usually a trifle larger although less sweetly scented. A distinct and ready means of identification is furnished by the long, narrow, lance-shaped leaves which grow from the root. Late in summer they send out many stolens or runners which take root at intervals and form new plants. These violets also bear cleistogamous flowers, tiny ones concealed among the bases of the leaves, which set their seed without unfolding. Consequently these plants are exceedingly well fitted to battle successfully for their existence. They require wetter situations than most blue violets and in such places greatly outnumber their blue cousins although their smaller size and modest colors render them inconspicuous by comparison.

YELLOW VIOLET.

Yellow Violets are much more local in their distribution than other species. They prefer rich but not moist woods and are most often found in small colonies along the banks of woodland brooks. They have always been prime favorites of mine because in a certain piece of woods where a small brook tumbles its noisy way over the stones down through the alders that line its banks, a colony of Yellow Violets has been established for a longer time than I can remember. The space occupied by them is barely larger than an ordinary room, but in this spot they grow in such profusion that the leaves hide the ground. This same place is an ideal one for migrating birds and the violets are always in bloom on May tenth when the season if migration is at its very height. Furthermore, in the alders, almost over my bed of violets, a pair of Wood Thrushes nearly always have their home. So whenever I see this species, it always brings to me memories of this favorite spot and of Wood Thrushes. There are two kinds of Yellow Violets, the downy and the smooth, the former having a hairy or downy stem and the latter having a number of basal leaves during its flowering season.

The Yellow Violet is one of the tallest members of the family, its stem ranging from six to eighteen inches in height. Usually two pairs of leaves branch out from the stem and from the axils grow the flower stalks. The two side petals of the handsome yellow flowers are heavily bearded and the lower one has prominent veinings leading down the throat. The markings are presumed to be guides for insects to follow to reach the nectar at the end of the short spur and the hairy beard is for them to hold to as they reach within and to force them to brush against the stigma and anthers in the proper manner. After the flowering season, the Yellow Violets have numerous small, closed, self-fertilizing blossoms on runners from the root.

PINK AZALEA; WILD HONEY-SUCKLE.

During early May, suitable rich woods, thickets and hillsides are aglow with the beautiful pink blossoms of Azalea. The rosy blush is the more prominent because the flowers commonly appear before or just as the leaves commence to grow. Collectively, the blossoms make a most wonderful picture and each individual flower is also beautiful in form and color. Considerable nectar is secreted at the base of the long flower tube, which is so filled with the long stamens and pistil that only long-tongued insects are able to reach the bottom. The bumblebee is an abundant and probably the most useful visitor. He first brushes against the very long, protruding style, the sticky end of which collects some pollen from his underparts, then clambers over the shorter stamens, dusting himself with fresh pollen before he gets at the desired sweets. That the handsome flower is but an advertisement to attract the useful insects is shown by the fact that soon after having been visited the whole corolla becomes loosened from the calyx and slips down to the end of the long style, where it hangs for a few days before falling to the ground.

Less common than the preceding species, is RHODORA which is shown in the lower half of the picture. This is a much lower shrub than Azalea, found in similar habitat but not as abundant anywhere. The corolla is long-tubed but instead of flaring out into even lobes, it has a three-notched, broad upper one and a smaller two-cleft lower lobe.

WHITE AZALEA or SWAMP HONEYSUCKLE is less common than the pink species and is chiefly confined to swamps near the coast. The flowers are quite similar to the others except that they are white, the tube is longer and the whole blossom is quite sticky. The flowers appear in June and July, long after the shrub is fully leaved.

MOUNTAIN LAUREL.

Some of our most famous paintings have been of homely and commonplace scenes; some of our most beautiful birds are reckoned as abundant; and it is the same with our wild flowers, although we are apt to regard most highly those species that are the most difficult to obtain. When I wish to see the most glorious floral panorama that Nature produces. I visit Laurel or Spoonwood swamps during the latter part of May. Great masses of beautiful pink and white blossoms top the handsome. dark-leaved shrubs. In favorable places where the soil is very rich. Laurel grows even more luxuriantly on wooded hillsides than in the more extensive swampy tracts. The stiff, oval. deep green leaves are evergreen and very decorative, so much so that great quantities of them are gathered for the making of wreaths, a practice that is gradually forcing one to make longer and longer journeys from the large cities if he wishes to see Mountain Laurel in its haunts.

Each individual flower is very interesting in form and structure. The buds are always pink and the opened flowers frequently are, the degree of pinkness depending upon the nature of the ground and the amount of light that is received by them. The corolla is saucer-shaped, with five points. A single short pistil rises in the center of the corolla, surrounded by ten stamens which are bent outward so that their tips are caught in little pockets provided for them; these little pockets also contain the fine pollen grains. If we touch one of the stamens on a mature flower, ever so lightly, snap,—it is released from its pocket and springs forward, throwing out its little load of pollen. Each blossom then, has ten spring guns all set and ready to be discharged as soon as a visiting bee touches them. As the winged creature visits the next flower some of the pollen that is dusted on the under surface of his body touches the stigma of the pistil even before his feet have disturbed its stamens enough to discharge them.

SHEEP LAUREL; LAMBKILL.

On moist hillsides and in fields we may find patches of the smaller, low-growing laurel, known as SHEEP LAUREL. The individual flowers are fully as pretty or perhaps more beautiful than those of Mountain Laurel as they are of a very bright and particularly handsome shade of pink. but the shrub itself and the flower masses are far inferior to the preceding in point of beauty.

Very abundant in mountains from Pennsylvania southwards, but of very local occurrence within our range is the GREAT LAUREL or RHOD-ODENDRON. In its southern haunts

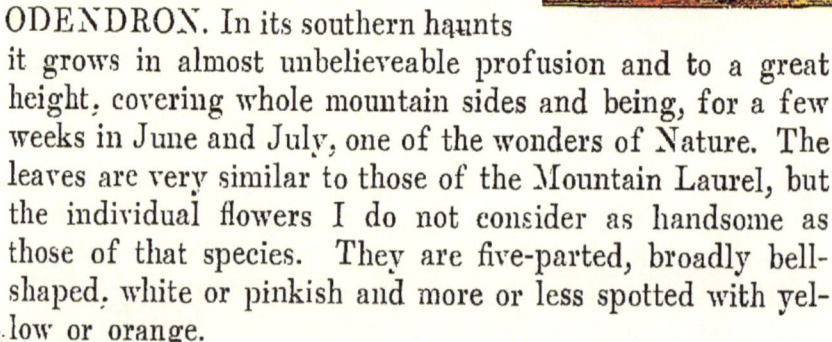

it grows in almost unbelieveable profusion and to a great height. covering whole mountain sides and being, for a few weeks in June and July, one of the wonders of Nature. The leaves are very similar to those of the Mountain Laurel, but the individual flowers I do not consider as handsome as those of that species. They are five-parted, broadly bell-shaped. white or pinkish and more or less spotted with yellow or orange.

Although the nectar of the laurels apparently is not injurious to the insects that partake of it, honey made by bees feeding upon it is slightly poisonous and the leaves of all species are quite poisonous to all animals that eat them.

The famous TRAILING ARBUTUS or MAYFLOWER, which also belongs to this same Heath Family, grows, as nearly everyone knows, on rocky hillsides or in woods. particularly under evergreen trees. Few flowers are as fragrant as are these little pink and white beauties that brave the raw weather of March and April and whose odor is very suggestive of that of the Water Lily. Unfortunately, Arbutus is yearly becoming less abundant owing to the great quantities that are gathered and to the fact that the pickers pull the vines up root and all.

HEDGE BINDWEED; WILD MORNING GLORY.

This attractive flower belongs to the Convolvulus Family, a small group of climbing or twining plants having regular, perfect bell or funnel-shaped flowers. Trailing through any wayside hedges, thickets or along old fences or walls, we are apt to find Wild Morning Glory firmly embracing the object of its support. In one large swamp I have found this plant showing a marked preference for climbing the stalks of Turk's-cap Lilies, which grow there in profusion, with the result that the strangle hold secured by the present species usually results in the distortion, wilting or death of the supporting plant. Bindweed is a plant of very rapid growth and is said to often make a complete turn in its left-handed spiral within two hours.

The flowers, at least until after they have been fertilized, open only during sunlight or sometimes during bright moonlight, at such times as their long tongued insect benefactors are apt to be abroad. It is probably that its most useful visitors are some of the sphinx moths that visit it after dark. Each of the five white stripes that alternate with the pink ones on the corolla of the flowers, lead to a nectary in the base, entrance to which is gained only through long tubes, thus preventing short-tongued insects, not capable of benefitting the flower, from partaking of its sweets. This ornamental plant remains in bloom from June until September.

COMMON DODDER is closely related to the last species but in addition to the climbing and twining tendencies of the latter, it is wholly parasitic and derives all its sustenance from the juices of its victims. Starting from a tiny seed the plant grows up the stem of a neighboring plant, develops little "suckers" that penetrate the bark of its foster parent, its roots wither away and it lives ever after upon its unfortunate victim. The stem is leafless, yellowish-orange and bears tiny bell-shaped whitish flowers.

GREAT MULLEIN.

The Common or Great Mullein, which is shown at the left on the opposite picture, is one of the commonest plants along our roadsides and in dry, rocky fields. In spring, tiny velvety leaves first appear, these gradually increasing in size until they become quite large and spread out in a rosette on the ground. From the middle of this rosette appear a tiny stalk which also keeps increasing in size and length until finally the summit may be from two to seven feet above ground. A few smaller leaves alternate in erect positions along this stalk. At the summit is a long spike

of green buds which open a few at a time and very irregularly into pretty five-parted bright yellow flowers. These stalks stand all through the fall and winter months as silent watchers over the barren fields. Even though classed only as a weed, it is a very handsome one, visited by many bees and the summit used by many a Kingbird as a convenient lookout perch. Children find many uses in their play from the soft, woolly leaves and in former times mild decoctions were also made from them for the relief and possible cure of throat troubles.

MOTH MULLEIN, also found in neglected or waste places, is tall but slender and apparently rather frail,— quite different from the stocky, powerful species last described. The flowers are shown at the right in the illustration on this page. They are larger and handsomer than the last, the bright orange-tipped stamens being quite prominent. A very loose cluster of buds appears at the top of the stalk and only one or two of them open each day, remaining open only for the one day.

The leaves, which seldom are present during the flowering season, are rather small and erect, and have notched or toothed edges. They have not the woolly texture of the last species but are smooth. Although known as Moth Mullein, it is believed that bees are the most frequent agents for fertilizing the blossoms.

TOADFLAX; BUTTER-AND-EGGS.

Although an immigrant from Europe, pretty Toadflax which is shown on the right hand of the opposite picture, has multiplied and spread, like the English Sparrow, until it is now found throughout our country from the Atlantic to the Pacific Oceans. Even without the blossoms, it is an attractive and decorative plant, the closely set, narrow, grayish-green leaves furnishing an agreeable contrast to the other foliage. It usually grows in such dense colonies that the effect produced is a very pleasing one.

The flowers grow in a spike at the top of the plant, each tubular, yellow blossom having a two-lipped corolla, the upper one being of two lobes and the lower of three, the central one of which extends back into a slender spur and has a protruding, pouting, orange palate that closes the throat of the flower. This arrangement, which is designed especially for the bumblebee, effectually closes the entrance to the interior to all light-weight bees and ants, but the weight of the bumblebees, together with his strength, easily forces the lips apart and he can partake of the nectar at his leisure. It is not at all difficult for one to see why the name of Butter-and-eggs should have been applied to this plant, the palate being just the color of an egg yolk and the rest of the flower the color of good butter.

BLUE TOADFLAX is a smaller species growing in sandy soil. It is not nearly as sturdy a species as the preceding, in fact the slender stem is ofttimes too weak to stand erect and the pretty blue blossoms are literally dragged in the dust. Both small butterflies and bees visit the little blossoms, which are too weakly constructed to prevent the sweets being drained even if they wished to. The name Toadflax is an opprobrious one applied to these plants because before the flowers appear the foliage is somewhat like that of the true flax.

PAINTED CUP; INDIAN PAINT BRUSH.

Although, at a casual glance, one would not suspect it, this plant belongs to the Figwort Family, as well as the species of toadflax and the mulleins. The reddish stem rises from a basal tuft of leaves and is also set with three to five-cleft leaves. The tiny greenish-yellow flowers at the summit of the stem are concealed by scarlet tipped, three-cleft bracts. Depending upon the nature of the soil and the amount of light received, the bracts are sometimes yellow-tipped and less often may be wholly green. Painted Cup grows in moist sandy soil in meadows or thickets and is quite local in its distribution. It is somewhat parasitic in its habits, its roots often attaching themselves to those of other nearby plants and stealing some of the juices they are storing up for their own use.

FALSE FOXGLOVE is a very pretty plant growing in dry sandy thickets or woods, that has similar parasitic tendencies, attaching its roots by little disks or suckers to the fine roots of trees or those of other plants. The beautiful pale yellow flowers, arranged in pairs loosely along the upper part of the stem, are nearly two inches in length. The corolla is bell-shaped, with five spreading lobes, five orange-tipped stamens and a protruding sticky-tipped pistil which receives pollen from a previous flower, from the bodies of incoming bees. The construction of these blossoms is such that bees always enter them upside down in order to be able to reach the nectar in the base; therefore they get the pollen which is released from the anthers by the pressure of their bodies, on their underparts where it is in just the right position to be implanted on the stigma of the next flower they visit. The leaves grow oppositely upon the stem, the upper ones being smooth edged and the lower ones toothed or lobed.

BLUETS; INNOCENTS.

From April until July, large beds of pretty little Bluets often transform our green fields into misty, bluish-white areas. While they are so very abundant that little attention is usually given them, these little flowers are quite interesting. They are dimorphic, that is different flowers are differently constructed. Some have a long, two-parted pistil that comes even to the end of the tiny little bell-shaped corolla and the anthers or polen sacs are located in pairs near the bottom of the tube; other blossoms have a very short pistil and the anthers are on opposite sides near the outer end of the tube. This is a very clever arrangement for insuring that pollen from the one kind of flower shall be left on the stigma of the other kind, which is usually on an entirely different plant. A bee visiting a high-anthered flower receives pollen near the base of his tongue and it can only be left at a plant which has flowers with a high stigma. The same is true of the flowers in which the anthers are low in the tube. An inspection of several clumps of these flowers will readily disclose the two kinds of blossoms, the differences being plainly evident in the shapes of the outside of the tube.

PARTRIDGEBERRY belongs to the Madder Family, as do bluets, and has dimorphic flowers like those of the last species. The vine trails along the ground, putting out its handsome round, dark green, white-veined leaves in pairs. The pinkish-white, four-lobed, bell-shaped flowers also grow in pairs at the ends of the stems and branches. They are not only beautiful but nearly as sweet scented as Arbutus. In fall the flowers are replaced by a single twinberry bright red in color. These berries last through the winter, provided they are not sooner eaten by birds, and the leaves are evergreen too.

CORAL or TRUMPET HONEY-SUCKLE.

This is a very ornamental woody vine growing from eight to fifteen feet in length, climbing over bushes or twining about the branches of young trees. The leaves are arranged oppositely, the lower ones having short stems, while those near the ends of the branches clasp the stem and are united at their bases. The form of the flowers and the terminal leaves is shown in the opposite illustration.

As is well known, red is the favorite color of our tiny Ruby-throated Hummingbird and we find that this bird is one of the flower's chief visitors and about the only one capable of reaching the nectar at the end of the long slender tube. In a wild state, Coral Honeysuckle is locally distributed in southern New England and New York but is very abundant in southern states. In fall, each flower is replaced by an orange colored berry, these berries being eaten by migrating birds and thus the seeds often scattered far and wide from the place of their growth. This is one of Nature's surest schemes to insure the starting of new colonies of plants.

WILD WHITE HONEYSUCKLE, which is naturalized from Europe, grows very abundantly in the south and is of local occurrence in tangled thickets in southern New England and New York. It is an agile climber, often twining its way up trees to the height of forty or more feet. Seated in clusters in the cup formed by the united terminal pair of leaves are the handsome and very fragrant flowers. The corolla tube is white within and pinkish or yellow on the outside, spreading into two lips, the upper of which has four lobes and the lower one being narrow and curved downward. The pistil and five stamens are very long and protrude far beyond the confines of the corolla. Its seeds are spread by migrating birds which eat the bright red berries that adorn it in fall.

CARDINAL FLOWER.

As the Scarlet Tanager is among the brightest and most glorious of our birds, so the Cardinal Flower is among our wild flowers. The gorgeous red blossoms are so very attractive that few can pass them by, with the result that the constant picking is rendering this species more difficult to find each year. The tall straight stem is rather closely set with alternating, toothed-edged leaves and the summit is, during August and September, topped with the beautiful spike of flowers as shown in the opposite illustration. The preferred habitat of the Cardinal Flower is moist or low ground, especially along small streams. If we wait patiently near some of the flowers we are quite sure to see visiting it. that little winged jewel that the flower too awaits, the Ruby-throated Hummingbird. As he poises on humming wings, before each flower in turn, he easily sips the nectar from the very base of the long slender tube and at the same time fulfills the life mission of the flower by setting its seed.

GREAT LOBELIA is almost a duplicate of the Cardinal Flower except that its flowers are blue and are less delicately and gracefully formed. Even though it may suffer by comparison in point of beauty. it is far more abundant in its chosen retreats on moist land or beside brooks. The reason is not difficult to discover for does it not flaunt the favorite color of the bees, its greatest benefactors, and bees are very common while Hummingbirds, upon which the Cardinal chiefly depends for its fertilization are comparatively rare. This also explains why it is that we have such a small number of brilliant red wild flowers. The stigmas of these flowers mature later than the anthers on the same blossoms; consequently it is necessary that pollen from later plants be brought by bees to those on which the stigma are in a receptive mood.

GOLDENRODS.

Goldenrods and in fact all the flowers on the following pages belong to that greatest of all plants families, the Composites. These have the small tubular flowers grouped in large heads and frequently surrounded by conspicuous rays for the express purpose of attracting insect visitors. The Goldenrod shown in the opposite picture is Early Goldenrod and is also quite similar to Canada Goldenrod, both of which species are among the most abundant of this most prolific genus. Goldenrods are very decorative and this species is one of the most graceful of them all, the flowering spikes curving in the most artistic manner. The flowers have eight or ten tiny golden-yellow rays. This species is abundant along roadsides and in dry fields and woods.

LANCE-LEAVED GOLDENROD is easily recognized because lance-shaped leaves are very closely crowded along the stem and the flowers are grouped in a large flat-topped cluster. This species is also occasionally known as Bushy Goldenrod and again as Fragrant Goldenrod, the latter because the crushed leaves and flowers are quite fragrant. It blooms very abundantly during the fall months in fields, woods or along the roads.

BLUE-STEMMED GOLDENROD is a rather slender species with toothed leaves alternating along the whole length of the stem and with short spikes of yellow flowers growing from the axils of the upper leaves. The individual flowers are larger than those of the proceding species and have three to five comparatively long golden rays. This species too is very common, especially so in woods.

SILVER-ROD or WHITE GOLDENROD, also a slender species, with the flowers evenly clustered in an oblong terminal spike, is the only one of the genus with white, or rather creamy-white flowers. In fact it is so different from the usual goldenrods that it requires more than a casual glance to identify it as such.

THE ASTERS.

Like goldenrods most of the asters bloom in fall and also like the last species they are very strong numerically. The flowers heads are composed of a central disk of numerous yellowish, tubular florets surrounded by strap-shaped flowers or rays. These flower heads are rarely single and often occur in great numbers on a single plant.

SMOOTH ASTERS, which is the species shown here, are abundant in dry soil and are in bloom from August until October. The ray florets are of a particularly handsome shade of blue. The plant is quite branching and the flower heads exceedingly numerous. It is particularly distinguished from other varieties by the fact that the leaves clasp the stem with a distinctly heart-shaped base.

NEW ENGLAND ASTER are one of the largest of this genus, attaining heights of two to six feet. The leaves are smooth-edged and lance-shaped. The flowers are rather large and purple rather than blue, containing thirty or forty rays about the golden center.

MANY-FLOWERED ASTER is rightly named for the flower heads are almost innumerable. The plant is very branching or bushy and each branch terminates in clusters of numerous but small flower head with white rays.

WOOD ASTERS have comparatively few flower heads, the centers are brownish yellow and the rays long, white, narrow and few in number. The leaves of this species are larger than those of the many-flowered species.

GOLDEN ASTERS abound in summer in dry sandy soil particularly near the sea coast. They are low branching species seldom attaining a height of more than a foot. The numerous flowerheads have brownish centers and bright orange-yellow rays. All asters are fertilized by bees or other visitors crawling over the central disk of florets.

BLACK-EYED SUSAN; CONE-FLOWER.

The bright orange and purple heads of these pretty flowers may be seen in many of our fields from the latter part of May until September. The hairy stems, which grow one or two feet in height, are exceedingly tough and difficult to break with the hands. The leaves, too, are hairy and very rough to the touch. This species is an original native of the western states and is one of the very few plants that have travelled from the west to the east in our country. Each stem is simple and unbranched but several of them often spring from the same root, each terminating in a single large showy blossom.

The conical, dark purple center is composed of long tubular florets that ripen in successive rings about the cone, a fringe of yellow pollen showing which ones are matured. The orange-yellow rays are neutral, with neither stamens nor pistils. They have their use, however, in attracting to the flowers, bees and butterflies to feast upon the nectar and the pollen.

ROBIN'S PLANTAIN is one of the earliest of the Composites to bloom, because of which it is sometimes called the Blue Spring Daisy. Most of the leaves are spatulate in shape and form a rosette at the base of the stem; a few other smaller ones clasp the stem alternately, diminishing in size until they reach the small cluster of flowers at the top of the stem. The central disks are dull yellowish and the numerous narrow rays are a pale purplish-blue. Both stem and leaves are very fuzzy. It is a common plant either in dry or moist soil, in fields or in woods and blooms during May and June. The rootstock is perennial, new plants springing up from the same every year, which together with the new ones soon form large colonies.

JERUSALEM ARTICHOKE.

This is an interesting native plant often known as the Wild Sunflower. Indians and early colonists used its tuberous roots much as we use potatoes today. It was also carried abroad and cultivated extensively, particularly in Italy, where it was known as Girasole Articocco (Sunflower Artichoke), from which name it was corrupted into the Jerusalem Artichoke as we know it now. The stalk, which grows from six to twelve feet in height is very rough and the three-ribbed, toothed-edged leaves, the lower ones of which are set oppositely on the stalk, are also rough,—this roughness presumably being to discourage crawling insects from reaching the summit. The several flower heads are two or three inches across and consist of from a dozen to twenty rays about a greenish-yellow center. This species naturally grows in somewhat moist thickets but is often seen in or about old gardens where it continues to grow as a reminder of the days when it was cultivated for food.

COMMON SUNFLOWER as a wild plant is native to the western half of the United States. The flower heads normally grow but from three to six inches in diameter, but under cultivation they often attain a mammoth size. They are grown for their ornamental beauty and also for the sake of the numerous seeds produced in the central disk. These seeds form a staple diet for most species of parrots. Goldfinches like them too, and pay frequent visits to gardens that contain them. Many bird lovers plant sunflowers just for the sake of attracting and feeding these birds during the winter months. Although sunflowers are now grown in nearly all civilized countries, they all originally came from America. Several other similar species occur in our range, nearly all being found in low meadows, thickets or swamps.

BEGGAR-TICKS; STICK-TIGHT.

One does not have to be a botanist or even a lover of flowers to know Beggar-ticks. Anyone who tramps woods and fields in fall is apt to at any moment find his clothes bristling with the little black, two-hooked seeds. They are well named "Stick-tight" for it is absolutely impossible to brush them off; they must be picked from the clothing one by one. They give anyone a very practical demonstration of the methods that some plants use to distribute their seeds in new localities, although the chances are that the victim as he plucks and casts them away does not realize that he is doing just what the plant had planned for him to do, found new colonies.

Beggar-ticks is shown by the picture on the left hand. It is a very branching or bushy species, attaining height of two to eight feet. The prominently veined and toothed leaves are quite handsome but the flowers, seated in a little terminal rosette of leaves are small and inconspicuous, just a few very short, tiny rays surrounding the small clusters of brownish florets which later will be the "ticks."

BUR-MARIGOLD or BROOK SUNFLOWER belongs to the same genus and has the same disagreeable habit of attaching its seeds to clothing or fur of animals. The flower heads, however, are quite handsome as they measure nearly two inches across and are composed of eight or ten broad yellow rays about the brownish-yellow center. Bur-Marigold is shown at the right in the illustration on this page.

COMMON WHITE DAISIES, although naturalized from Europe, are one of our commonest field flowers. They need no description for who does not remember having his fortune told by plucking one by one the white rays that surround the golden center. Equally abundant is TANSY with its aromatic, finely divided leaves and rayless yellow flower heads.

PASTURE THISTLE.

This is the thistle that we most often see in fields and pastures. It is one of the largest species, the flower heads often measuring three inches across and usually with only one or two flowers on a single plant. The stem is stout and straight and from one to two feet tall. The alternating leaves are jagged-edged and armed with very sharp prickles as is also the large involucre that contains the pink florets. The object of all this armor is to make it difficult for and to discourage crawling insects from gaining the top of the plant. The Pasture Thistle is the species shown in the opposite picture.

CANADA THISTLES, so called, are in reality waifs that have strayed across the ocean and have multiplied and become very numerous throughout our range. This species grows from one to three feet in height. The stem is slender and quite branching and at the end of each branch are many small flower heads measuring but little over an inch across. The leaves, too, are much more slender than those of the preceding species but have just as many and just as sharp prickles. After maturing each of the florets is replaced by a small seed with a silky parachute on which it can float away to new pastures. The seeds are eaten by birds, particularly goldfinches which also work considerable of the downy plumes into the lining of their nests.

DANDELIONS also are included in the great Composite Family. They grow almost anywhere and everywhere, particularly on lawns or in other places where they are not wanted. Everyone is familiar with their rosettes of jagged leaves and with the handsome flowerheads composed of golden-yellow, strap-shaped florets, each perched at the summit of a hollow stem. The yellow flowers are replaced within a few days by a round misty ball of seeds and their parachutes. ready to be blown far away at the slightest breath of air.

Bibliographic sources :

Wild flowers of New York (1912)

Author: Reed, Chester A. (Chester Albert), 1876-1912

Publisher: Mohonk Lake, N.Y. : Mohonk Salesrooms

This documentary study use,
combined in various proportions,
elements from the following categories,
forms and subsets :
- fair use
- documentary
- documentary photography
- feature
- journalism
- arts journalism
- visual journalism
- photojournalism
- celebrity photography
in order to :
- employ material as the object of cultural critique ,
- quote to illustrate an argument or point ,
- use material in historical sequence,
providing independent opinion,
using photos, press articles, advertisements,
opinions of fans etc. ...